Dear Calvin

Story by Chris McTrustry

Illustrations by
Tom Jellett

Rigby PM Plus Chapter Books
part of the Rigby PM Program
Ruby Level

U.S. edition © 2003 Rigby Education
Harcourt Achieve Inc.
10801 N. MoPac Expressway
Building #3
Austin, TX 78759
www.harcourtachieve.com

Text © 2003 Thomson Learning Australia
Illustrations © 2003 Thomson Learning Australia
Originally published in Australia by Thomson Learning Australia

10 9 8 7 6 5 4 3 2
08

Dear Calvin
    ISBN 0 75786 890 8

Printed in China by 1010 Printing International Ltd

Contents

Chapter 1 *Miles and Miles from London* 4

Chapter 2 *London (At Last!)* 9

Chapter 3 *At the Game!* 13

Chapter 4 *Appointment Day* 16

Chapter 5 *The Famous Dr. Khan* 19

Chapter 6 *Tests* 22

Chapter 7 *An Operation* 25

Chapter 8 *Still in the Hospital* 28

Chapter 9 *Coming Home!* 31

Miles and Miles from London

Jumbo Jet
April 14

Dear Calvin,

The plane on the postcard that I am including with this letter is exactly the same as the plane I'm **flying** in right now. Dad helped me mark an X to show you where we're sitting. I **love** flying! There are movies and computer games and videos and snacks. It's cool! I go for a stroll every now and then to stretch my legs. Dad says that it's good for my circulation.

I've had my dinner and my medicine. I'm sick of taking it. (That was a joke. Get it?) Dad's asleep. He missed the second movie — a kissing one (yuck) — and almost missed dinner.

I wish you and Mom were coming with us to London. It would be so exciting if we were all going there for a vacation, instead of just Dad and I going to see a doctor.

I'll write again soon.

Love,

Ben

P.S. Don't let Groucho bark too much. Mr Kontaris might complain.

Bangkok Airport
Miles and miles and
miles from London
April 15

Dear Calvin,

I **hate** flying.

When the pilot announced that we were landing, I thought we were in London. **Wrong!** We're not even half way there yet! We're in Bangkok, in the terminal (that's a huge waiting room with stores and stuff), waiting for the plane to refuel and the new passengers to get on board. Guess how long that will take? **Two hours!**

Two hours to put fuel in a plane! What's the deal with that? Imagine if it took two hours to put gas in our car! Formula One racing cars can get refueled in seven seconds! Looks like I'll just have to be patient. (Huh! I know all about being a "patient," don't I, Calvin? Ha ha!)

If you look at the picture on this postcard that I'm including, you'll see a black X. I'm almost 68% positive that's where we are sitting.

Yes! Got to go now! They just announced that it's time to board our flight. Dad is sorting out boarding passes and passports. I'll mail this letter here at the airport (I'd better hurry!), and I'll write again soon.

Love,

Ben

P.S. Tell Groucho and Mom that I miss them already.

Chapter 2

London (At Last!)

Heathrow Airport
London
April 15

Dear Calvin,

We're in London! At last. I didn't think we'd ever get here. The flight from Bangkok took forever. I know flying **sounds** exciting, but you don't see much when you're so high up — especially when it's cloudy. At least I saw some of London as the plane got closer to the airport.

Now we're down again, on English ground, and the view isn't much better. Gray. Concrete. Clouds.

But guess what . . . we'll be riding in a black London taxi to our hotel! Cool, eh? It should be fun driving through London's streets. I wonder if I'll see the Queen!

Bye for now.
Love to you and Mom,
Ben

Dear Calvin,

Dad and I rode on a bus just like the one in this picture. And do you know whose house we passed? The Queen's. Yep. The one and only. I waved as we went past Buckingham Palace. You never know — she might have been looking out of a window. Maybe she saw me.

11

Dear Calvin

I'm off to see some doctors this afternoon. Dad thinks they'll be able to help me. I hope so. This is the first time since we left home that Dad has talked about me being sick. Up until now he's acted like we've just come here for a vacation.

Dad said he's got a surprise for me. He's going to tell me what it is after we see the doctors. I wonder what it will be.

I wish you and Mom were here with me. Give Groucho a pat for me.

Lots of love,

Ben

Chapter 3
At the Game!

The Hotel
April 17

Dear Calvin,

Guess where we went this afternoon? To the soccer game at Upton Park! Yep, **that** was Dad's surprise. It was pretty cool — you know how much I love the West Ham team. I can't believe I was actually at Upton Park!

Dad says we'll be going out to dinner tonight with his aunt and uncle. He says that Uncle Albert and Aunt Isabel are my great uncle and great aunt. So how does he know I'll think they're so great? What if they're just OK? (Ha ha!) So until dinner I'll tell you about the game.

It was the West Ham United team against the Manchester United team. Everybody around us was cheering for West Ham. We kept yelling "Go Hammers!"

The Hammers offense was incredible. They scored early in the game and then again just before half-time. It was 2 – 0 at the half. In the second half Manchester scored on a penalty kick, but the Hammers shut them down for the rest of the game.

Dad kept looking at me and asking, "Are you warm enough?" He must have asked me that forty times! And, "Are you comfortable?" I wish he wouldn't worry so much. I'm OK. But the sooner the doctors work out some treatment, the better! I can't wait until I'm well again, so that I can play soccer with you and with my team.

Love,

Ben

P.S. You and Mom will have to look for us in the crowd when this game is shown on the TV back home. I made sure we waved – a lot.

Chapter 4

Appointment Day

The hotel
April 18

Dear Calvin,

I'm off to the hospital again today. I have to meet another doctor — Dr. Khan. He's a really important doctor. Dad is sure that he'll be able to help me. My appointment is later this morning, so I'll tell you and Mom about our dinner with Uncle Albert and Aunt Isabel while I'm waiting to go.

We went to a "posh" restaurant. That's what Uncle Albert called it. He's funny. He kept telling jokes and "finding" coins in my ears! I had Yorkshire pudding — even though we're in London.

Aunt Isabel held my hand all through dinner. (That made it really hard to cut up my food. Ha, ha!) She kept telling me how wonderful it was to finally meet me, and that I was "a grand lad." She was really nice. It was a fun night.

The picture that I'm sending is of Big Ben, London's famous clock. We saw it the other day, when we went to the Houses of Parliament.

Did you know that a guy named Guy Fawkes (A guy named Guy!) once tried to blow up the Houses of Parliament? Don't worry — he was stopped, and it was a long, long time ago (even before Grandma and Grandpa were born). Now every November, the English celebrate Guy Fawkes Day by lighting bonfires and setting off fireworks.

Dad has been really quiet this morning. I think he's nervous about meeting a famous doctor like Dr. Khan. I am too. I just hope Dr. Khan will be able to help me.

Oh, oh. Here comes Dad. It's time to go. Bye for now.

Love,

Ben

P.S. Hi, Mom. I miss you.

Chapter 5

The Famous Dr. Khan

Gloucester Hotel
London
April 19

Dear Calvin,

The soldiers in the picture I'm sending are called the Royal Household Cavalry. They ride their horses through the middle of London every day. They ride through all the cars and buses and trucks and taxis (there are **lots** of taxis) from their stables to Whitehall Palace. We saw the Household Cavalry when we were on the way to Dr. Khan's office yesterday.

But I suppose you and Mom will want to know how my appointment went. OK — big breath. Dr. Khan said that I'll have to go into the hospital for special tests, then he'll be able to decide the best way to treat me. I might have to have an operation. Dad looked pretty upset when Dr. Khan told us that.

Dr. Khan was really nice, and laughed a lot, but the thing I remember most about him was his hands. They were so big and strong.

Dad says that we should stay in tonight and rest up, because tomorrow's the day I check in to the hospital. He says that I shouldn't worry. I should just think about getting home and seeing you and Mom again. No need to tell me that! I think about you two every day.

Love,
Ben

Chapter 6

Tests

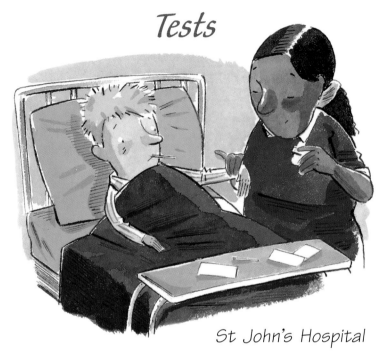

St John's Hospital
London
April 21

Dear Calvin,

Sorry I didn't write yesterday, but I was having the tests here at the hospital. They really hurt, Calvin. I cried. I couldn't help it. I know the nurses and doctors were trying to help me, but the needles and the other stuff really hurt.

Dad kept saying that I had to be brave. I really tried to be brave. And you know, I think I **was** brave, because I didn't get out of bed and run away. I wanted to, but I suppose the nurses would have caught me easily.

This is a picture of the hospital I'm in. Sorry there's no X to mark where I am, but I'm not really sure **where** I am. I feel sleepy most of the time. The nurses give me medicine (More medicine. I have to take **lots** of medicine.), and it makes me very tired.

Dad had his dinner with me tonight. He told me that all the tests are finished (Good!), and that the doctors expect to have the results soon. I know what the results will say — "Ben is sick." They should also say, "Ben is very sore after the tests and will not have to have any more needles — ever." Yeah, right.

I'm sorry, Calvin, but I can't write any more. My arm has a needle stuck in it. It doesn't hurt that much (Hey, I must be getting tougher!), but I'm feeling really tired.

Look after Mom, okay? I'll write again really soon.

Love,

Ben

Chapter 7

An Operation

St John's Hospital
London
April 23

Dear Calvin,

Dr. Khan says that tomorrow is **The Day**. He wants to operate on me! I knew I was sick, but I thought I'd come over here to London, and Dr. Khan — the smart, famous doctor — would give me some miracle medicine, and **pow!** I'd be cured. No. An operation. I don't know about that.

Dad was pretty upset today. I think he'd been crying. He sat beside my bed all day. I'd fall asleep, and every time I'd wake up, Dad would be there in **his** chair. No one else gets to sit in **his** chair – not even Aunt Isabel, when she and Uncle Albert come to visit.

Oh oh. There's a whole bunch of doctors and nurses coming my way. Maybe I should tell them that I've changed my mind and would like to go home.

Yeah. That's a good plan. I'll look Dr. Khan in the eye and just say, "Sorry, Dr. Khan, I've changed my mind and I'd like to go home."

Looks like I'm stuck here. Dr. Khan told me that all the doctors and nurses are ready to operate, so I'm not allowed to change my mind now. Guess I'll have to be brave. I told Dad I'd be brave, and he cried. Then I cried. I thought we would cry all night!

Gotta go. The nurse is telling me to get some sleep. As if I'll be able to sleep tonight!

Love to you and Mom,
Ben

Chapter 8

Still in the Hospital

St John's Hospital
London
May 2

Dear Calvin,

Well, I got through the operation all right. A doctor gave me a small needle, then told me to count backward from twenty. Easy, huh? Uh-uh. I only got as far as seventeen, I think, then I was fast asleep. Next thing I knew, I was back in my room. It was as if I'd just blinked. Dad told me that I'd been asleep for two whole days!

Sorry it's been so long since my last letter. I've been having all sorts of treatment. It makes me feel awful. But Dr. Khan says that I'll feel better before too long. If he wasn't such a smart, famous doctor, I probably wouldn't believe him.

I'm feeling really bad right now, so Dad is writing this letter for me. That explains why the handwriting is so bad! (Very funny, Ben.) And I have no fun pictures to send to you and Mom.

I've lost a lot of weight, so I'll have to eat a lot when I get home. I can't wait to go home. I miss everyone.

love,

Ben

P.S. Calvin, tell Mom that I miss her, too.

Dad

Chapter 9
Coming Home!

Heathrow Airport
London
June 3

Dear Calvin,

Can you guess what the plane in this picture means? Yes! We're coming home! We're at the airport now. Only two hours until we board the plane. I can't wait.

Uncle Albert and Aunt Isabel are here with us. They picked us up at our hotel and drove us to the airport. They've both made me promise to come back and visit them when I'm a little older. I'll have to get a part-time job. Airfares to England aren't cheap, you know.

I can't wait to see you and Mom. I hope you won't mind if we don't play soccer too soon. I'm still a little weak. Dad says I'll be better in no time. But just how long is no time? It's been weeks since my operation, and I still feel lousy! But at least I'll be home soon.

Lots of love,
Your (getting better, really fast) brother,
Ben
P.S. My haircut is a teeny bit different from the last time you saw me. I'm kind of bald. Don't laugh too much, okay?
P.P.S. Hi, Mom. See you real soon!